20th Century Defences in Britain
Cambridgeshire

including Peterborough
and Huntingdon

Mike Osborne was born in London, but hs lived on the Cambridgeshire border for 25 years. He worked in Cambridgeshire until he took early retirement in 1997. A member of the Fortress Study Group, and the Airfield Research Group, he has published material on Civil War fortifications, and Second World War defences, including a companion volume to this one, on Lincolnshire. Between 1995 and 2000, he co-ordinated contributions to the Defence of Britain Project in ten eastern counties.

20th Century Defences in Britain
in Britain

Cambridgeshire

Dr Mike Osborne

CONCRETE PUBLICATIONS

Published by Concrete Publications

45 Church Street
Market Deeping
Lincolnshire
PE6 8AN

British Library Cataloguing in Publication Data:
A catalogue record is available from the British Library.

ISBN 0-9540378-0-4

Copyright © Dr Mike Osborne

Printed by
St Edmundsbury Press

CONTENTS

I INTRODUCTION

The study of twentieth century military remains is accompanied by its own particular challenge. As the subject gains respectability amongst the archaeological establishment, and the documentary and archive underpinning emerges, the actual evidence on the ground continues to disappear. This has been going on for many years, but a combination of natural decay, military cutback and commercial development is accelerating the process. At the same time as the written record is surfacing, the oral one

RAF Duxford: Building 80, World War 1 workshops and parachute store, said to have been used as a church as well.

is disappearing. Fortunately, a number of initiatives over the last twenty or so years, have sought to record both physical evidence, and memories, in order to ensure that as little as possible is lost for ever. As Richard Morris recently observed, we know more about Roman marching camps, than we do of the army camps which housed the troops involved in the D-Day landings.

The major initiative aimed at recording twentieth century military structures is the Defence of Britain Project. This grew out of a pilot study carried out by members of the Fortress Study Group, in Holderness,on the east Yorkshire coast. From this grew

Dog-in-a-Doublet: pillbox built by the County Council in 1939, and camouflaged.

8

RAF Brampton: surely the only thatched guardroom ever; this cottage ornee of c1820 was the gate-lodge to the early nineteenth century Brampton Park which became the HQ of the 8th US Army Air Force in 1942.

the notion for a national survey, supported by most of the major heritage and archaeological bodies. The Project proper began life in 1995 based on a loose network of volunteers, co-ordinated at regional level, and feeding in site records to a national database, supervised by a full-time director, and based at the Imperial War Museum at Duxford. Support for fieldwork was also provided, and the Council for British Archaeology, who oversaw the whole operation, also commissioned Colin Dobinson to carry out a comprehensive archive survey of all the material covering relevant topics such as anti-aircraft defences, the development of radar, and the preparations for D-Day.

9

Imperial War Museum, Duxford; a restored Allan-Williams turret from Essex.

Brampton Park: RAF and 8th USAAF HQ; subsequently RAF Strike Command, the Logistics Command HQ.

10

This operation, combining specialists, professionals, and up to 3000 volunteer recorders, had, in five years, made great inroads into the half-million or so sites estimated to exist. At the end of this first phase, it was decided to focus on anti-invasion defences in great detail, and to record all other military, and military-associated sites in less detail on a separate database. This process continues apace, supported by grants from the Heritage Lottery Fund, and both databases will be accessible to the general public through the Internet in time. As military archaeology as an emergent discipline continues to attract interest in the way that industrial archaeology has done over the last 45 years, it is vital that information is both recorded and disseminated. This process is reflected by increasing member ship of such groups as the Fortress

Cambridge: The Regional Seat of Government dating from the Cold War period.

Study Group, and the Airfield Research Group, by interest shown by local history societies, and by the inclusion of the topic in archaeology courses. The range of sites recorded by the Project is vast: from Edwardian coast defences to 1960's air defence missile systems; from hospitals or headquarters in stately homes, to prisoner-of-war camps and Land Army hostels, from pillboxes to Regional Seats of Government. Numbers, too, are enormous, up to 25000 pillboxes were built in the Second World War, as were nearly 800 airfields. the population sheltered in up to 500,000 air-raid shelters', every village had somewhere for the Home Guard to drill and train, in both world wars, extensive lengths of coastline were fortified, and enormous citizen armies were raised, equipped, trained, and shipped out by plane or ship to fight. Cambridgeshire has a representative share of many of these monuments. This book is intended both to inform, and to jog memories. Fresh information is still sought and will contribute to the overall width of the existing database. You can send information to

The Defence of Britain Project, The Imperial War Museum, Duxford Airfield, Duxford, Cambridgeshire, CB2 4OR

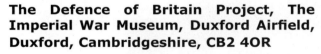

Aseries of county guides was embarked on in 1997, when Brasseys published volumes on KENT by David Burridge, and LINCOLNSHIRE by Mike Osborne. This present volume continues that series under a different imprint. It is intended that more will follow.

AIRFIELDS

Prior to the Great War, Cambridgeshire had witnessed pioneering developments both in flying, and in aircraft production. Early aviators were familiar visitors to Cambridge; in 1912 airships were involved in the Army's manoeuvres on Midsummer Common; and in Peterborough, Sages were building aero-

RAF Duxford: World War 1 coupled general service sheds, commonly referred to as 'Belfast Truss' hangars because of their roof structure; three pairs of these hangars remain; similar ones once stood at Fowlmere nearby.

planes. The combination of landscape and remoteness from the action made Cambridgeshire a perfect location for training and experiment. The army practised with spotter balloons and other forms of aerial reconnaissance, and flying training stations were set up by the Royal Flying Corps [RFC] at Wyton in 1916, Fowlmere in 1918, and at Duxford in 1919. Only Wittering was a truly operational station when, in late 1916 it became the base for one flight of 38 [Home Defence] Squadron equipped with BE2b's, the rest of the Squadron being based in south Lincolnshire. Their task was to intercept Zeppelins heading for both military and industrial targets around Lincoln, Nottingham, Derby and the Humber estuary. It was important that fighters were kept in the air as long

RAF Duxford: a World War 1 barrack block.

14

as possible, and a network of landing-grounds was established for pilots to land away from their home-base. Cottenham, Horseheath, Upwood, and Yelling are examples of such airfields. Alongside the fighters at Wittering, [or 'Stamford' as it was named until 1924] were the trainees of 1 Training Depot Station. At the end of the War a storage facility was established, and, in 1920 the station was put into care and maintenance. Few airfield buildings remain from this period. Whilst the hangars at Fowlmere were demolished in 1923, those at Duxford remain. These are Coupled General Service Sheds, commonly named for their characteristic roof construction as 'Belfast Truss' hangars. Also at Duxford are the church and a barrack block from this period. The site of Wyton's First War buildings can be deduced from surviving cottages along the A142 which predated them. In Church Street, Werrington, north of Peterborough, a single storey building, in use as a cottage but which was brought from RAF Scampton in Lincolnshire where it had been the Officers' Mess in the Great War stood until 2000. One of Wittering's early hangars was incorporated into the later layout and appears on the 1939 plans. In 1924 a review of the country's aerial defence needs found active roles for Duxford as the major fighter base in East Anglia, and for Wittering as home of the Central Flying School where instructors were trained.

By the 1930's the need for re-armament

THE
DEFENCE

OF
BRITAIN

RAF Peterborough: the Officers Mess of 1931.

was becoming more apparent and the RAF saw a big expansion. Peterborough [Westwood Farm] opened in 1931 as an Aircraft Storage Depot, served by a railway siding off the LNER line. Within a few years the Air Ministry identified a need for more trained pilots and Peterborough was chosen as the base for an Elementary Flying Training School. It had a grass field, an 'A'type hangar, and a collection of elegant neo-Georgian buildings as Officers' Mess, Sergeants' Mess, and Station HQ, all of which still stand. So ambitious was the RAF's expansion of the early 1930s that steps were taken to integrate new airfields into the landscape. Standard designs for each of the component buildings of an airfield, were submitted for the approval of the Fine Arts Commission,

16

RAF Bassingbourn: a 'C' type hangar of the Expansion Period

before being issued by the Air Ministry. Practicalities had their place alongside aesthetics, and provision was made in hangars and residential blocks alike for protection against bombing and against gas attack. The hangar most characteristic of this Expansion Period was the'C'type with gabled ends and a deep, sand-filled roof. Examples can be seen at Bassingbourn, Upwood, Wittering, and Wyton.

Civilian flying had come on apace too, and Marshall's Flying School Ltd. was set up on the family farm in 1930. In 1936 when the RAF Volunteer Reserve was created, Marshalls were contracted to run Elementary and Reserve Flying Training

17

Marshall's Cambridge Airport: The Control building of 1937.

Schools in both Cambridge and Oxford to which, amongst others, members of the Universities' Air Squadrons might transfer on completion of their basic tuition. When Marshalls moved their operations to their new aerodrome on Newmarket Road in 1937, No 22 E&RFTS moved as well to continue producing highly-trained pilots for the RAF. The Control building, Hangar 1, and the former aerodrome hotel, all survive from this period, unmistakeably Art Deco in their elegance.

RAF Duxford: airman's Barrack Block Type 'B' [protected].

RAF Duxford: the Expansion Period Airman's Mess.

RAF Oakington: a 'J' type hangar of c. 1939.

There are a number of Expansion Period stations in the county. Wyton [1935] was the first, and was built as a bomber base with a satellite station following in 1938 at Alconbury - the first such satellite in Britain. In 1937, Upwood opened, also for bombers, and a year later, another bomber base at Bassingbourn. From 1935 on, Wittering and Duxford were transformed into operational fighter stations. Alconbury was designed to accommodate aircraft dispersed from a parent airfield which would remain responsible for repairs and maintenance, so hangars were not deemed necessary. Four of the five main stations were given 'C' type hangars. Early in the War it was realised that many more bases were needed and so Molesworth [1940],

20

RAF Oakington: the interior of a 'J' type hangar; the conveniently parked double decker bus gives an idea of the size.

Oakington [1939] and Waterbeach [1940] were built for bombers. At these three stations can be seen 'J' type hangars which were more quickly and cheaply built than the more imposing 'C' types. However, all these stations share the other buildings designed in less pressured times. Examples of Messes, HQ buildings, water towers, residential accommodation, synthetic trainers, armouries, MT sections, and so on, can still be seen on all these sites. Just as hangars can give an indication of the date of an airfield so can control towers, or 'watch offices' as the RAF dubbed them. The two most characteristic types of the Expansion Period, were the 'Fort' [207/36 and 1959/34] and the

RAF Bassingbourn: the 207/36 'Fort' type watch office modified by the USAAF with the addition of another storey wrapped aroud the central tower; now a museum.

'Villa' [2328/39 and 5845/39]. A 'Fort' still stands at Bassingbourn, as do 'Villas' at Waterbeach and Wyton.

As the War took its course and the bomber offensive developed still more airfields were needed - Bottisham [1940], Bourn [1941], and Steeple Morden [1940] for bombers, and Castle Camps [1940] for fighters. With the arrival of the United

RAF Waterbeach: the 5845/39 'Villa' type brick-built watch office.

RAF Bassingbourn: the Expansion Period Parachute Store.

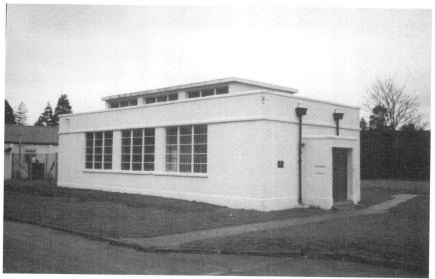

RAF Bassingbourn: the Expansion Period water-tower clad in brick to meet the recommendations of the Royal Fine Art Commission.

States 8th Army Air Force [8AAF], the demand increased significantly. During 1942 the existing stations at Alconbury, Bassingbourn, Bottisham, Molesworth and Steeple Morden were handed over for the use of 8AAF bombers and Duxford and Fowlmere for fighters. In addition, new bases were built for the 8AAF bomber groups at Glatton, Kimbolton and Little Staughton. To compensate the RAF for bases allocated to the Americans, and to

RAF Oakington: the temporary brick-built Navigation trainer.

RAF Wyton: the Dome trainer for AA gunners, one of only a handful to survive in the whole country.

RAF Sibson: a Bellman hangar removed here from Peterborough post-war.

enable them to meet new commitments, bomber bases were freshly built during 1941-2 at Gransden Lodge, Graveley, [a straight swap for Alconbury], Newmarket and Warboys. Even as late as 1943, new airfields were still in process of construction - Mepal, Witchford and Wratting Common for bombers. In addition there were airfields throughout the War fulfilling other more specialist roles such as Sibson, Peterborough and Caxton Gibbet for training, Snailwell for Army Co-operation, and Somersham for hush-hush work with Special Operation Executive [SOE] personnel to be flown into occupied Europe.

RAF Oakington: one of a pair of 'T2' hangars.

These wartime constructions were, in contrast to the elegance of the 1930-1940 construction, very much functional and utilitarian. The most common hangar design was now the 'T2' type- 'T' or 'transportable'. These could be erected by 12 men working flat-out for 20 days with everything going right. Such hangars were added to Duxford and Oakington, for instance, and constituted the primary provision at new airfields such as Graveley, Warboys and Witchford. There had been other attempts to design a cheap, easily-erected hangar, and Peterborough was given four Bellman hangars, one of which was moved to Sibson after the War and now houses small, private aircraft. At

RAF Wratting Common: the 'B1' hangar built on most wartime bomber stations as and aircraft repair shed.

Little Staughton can be seen small Robins hangars, and at Marshalls in Cambridge, some Blister hangars. The other large hangar often found on wartime airfields is the B1 which was generally used as an aircraft repair shed. The normal combination on a bomber field would be two T2s and a B1, and just such a pattern can still be seen at Wratting Common. For some reason, Newmarket has two B1 hangars. Most of the buildings on wartime airfields were of a temporary nature. This is clearly a relative term, as many are still going strong 50 years on. All sorts of hutting was developed but the commonest were the Temporary Brick - one brick in thickness, and the Nissen hut. All these

28

huts came in a variety of sizes and were grouped for particular functions. Thus the buildings of a peacetime station were reproduced on a wartime one but using utility constructions. Little Staughton's Technical Site can be seen virtually complete made up of a combination of Temporary Brick; [Night-flying Equipment Shed, Floodlight Tractor and Trailer Shed] Nissen Hut; [Fire-tender Shelter, Station Offices] Romney Hut; [Main Stores] and a few odd examples of Seco and of Butler. The lesson of dispersing aircraft to minimise air-raid damage had been painfully learned, so, just as hangars were dispersed on wartime airfields, then living accommodation was also grouped around the perimeter. Hence the little clusters of decaying Nissen and Temporary

RAf Duxford the 343/43 watch office, the most common wartime design.

RAF Little Staughton: the 13726/41 type watch office for bomber satellite airfields; a similar tower may be seen at Gransden Lodge.

Brick buildings still to be seen around Castle Camps and Warboys, for instance. Wartime Watch Offices were also built to new designs in Temporary Brick with stucco finish. Most bomber stations were given a square, two-storey type such as can be seen at Duxford, [12779/41 or 343/43 for all arms] or at Gransden Lodge and Little Staughton, [13726/41 for bomber satellites]. The oddest control tower in the county would appear to be that at Marshalls, currently in use, and looking suspiciously like a Bofors anti-aircraft tower.

One problem always around in the Eastern Counties is fog. One solution to this was

RAF Little Staughton: a 24 foot Nissen hut, probably Main Stores.

RAF Bottisham: a temporary brick hut, probably Squadron Offices.

Marshall's Cambridge Airport: Handcraft huts, a design more frequently found at Fleet Air Arm airfields.

RAF Waterbeach: the water tower.

RAF Little Staughton: a Robins type 'B' hangar, one of several on this site.

'Fido' which was a system by which petrol was piped along the side of a runway and its vapour ignited in order to clear fog and to create enough visibility for aircraft to land safely. The first station in Britain to be FIDO equipped was Graveley, and here were carried out the experiments which led to successful installation and operation on many other airfields. All of this going on whilst the resident Pathfinder squadron carried out its normal operations. The advent of the heavy bomber had necessitated the construction of concrete runways at most stations, but it must be remembered that some, such as Peterborough, never had runways. The usual pattern was a triange of three intersecting runways of between 1400 and 2000 yards. [1260-1800m] At Glatton,

Marshall's Cambridge Airport: a Blister hangar; another like it, on the opposite side of the airfield housed a fighter for airfield defence.

Marshall's Cambridge Airport: the post-war Control Tower which appears to be based on the design for a Bofors AAgun tower, found on airfields, factories and radar sites.

34

Brampton Grange: RAF 7 Group HQ, later 1st Air Division of 8th USAAF HQ.

Castle Hills House, Huntingdon: the adjacent District Council offices-'Pathfinder House', commemorate this as a wartime Bomber Command HQ.

RAF Lord's Bridge: a munitions shelter at this bomb and chemical wepons depot, served by a branch line.

Rose Court Farm was allowed to remain, marooned in the middle of the triangle - a unique situation. The dense concentration of establishments and units made both co-ordination and direction vital, and a number of Formation Headquarters were located in the County. Brampton Park became HQ for the 1st Air Division of the 8AAF, taking in with it Brampton Grange which had been RAF 7 Group HQ. Walcot Hall, south of Stamford was HQ of the US 67th Fighter Wing, as was Sawston Hall of the 66th. which included Duxford and Fowlmere. Castle Hills House in Huntingdon became HQ for RAF bomber forces in the area and is now known

36

Mepal: the L-shaped blastwalls of one of the three launching pads for THOR inter-contential ballastic missiles.

as Pathfinder House to commemorate particular units under its command. Other establishments contributed to the airborne effort. Lords Bridge, south-west of Cambridge, now the University Observatory, was a munitions depot for the 8AAF, storing bombs and chemicals, and served by a railway link, now disappeared. At Horsey Toll between Peterborough and Whittlesey was a Maintenance Unit, and an Aviation Fuel Depot was located in brick-pits near Farcet. A large RAF Hospital was established in Ely with buildings echoing the grandest of the Expansion Period.

Ely: the water-tower of the Expansion Period RAf hospital, now civilian.

After the War many stations reverted almost immediately to agriculture. Some continued to fulfil front-line roles in the Cold War, such as Mepal which was revitalised in the 1950s as a THOR inter-continental ballistic missile site. Molesworth gained notoriety in the 1980s as a CRUISE Missile base. Now, in a new Millennium, a variety of fates have overtaken the County's 29 formerly active

38

**Ely: the art deco lines of the wards of the
RAF hospital, now civilian.**

airfields. Bassingbourn and Waterbeach
are in the hands of the army - recruit
training and Royal Engineers airfield
construction unit respectively. Marshalls is
still a flourishing civil airport, and carries
out large-scale aeronautical engineering
work alongside. Glatton [now known as
Connington] is a civil airport for
Peterborough. Molesworth and Alconbury
continue in US Air Force use. Sibson
trains parachutists and hosts private fliers.
Wyton and Brampton, between them,
comprise the RAF Logistics Command.
Little Staughton, Witchford, Warboys, and
Bourn are industrial or trading estates.
Most of the rest have returned to
agriculture, although there are airfield
buildings visible at all of them. The two

39

exceptions are Duxford which is part of the Imperial War Museum, and Wittering which remains an operational RAF station.

RAF Alconbury: Gate-guard and Baptist Church.

AIR DEFENCE

The major threat from the air during the Great War was from airships, and it was the job of the Home Defence squadrons to intercept and destroy the Zeppelins as near to the coast as possible before any damage could be done to inland targets. Parts of one of these - No 38 Squadron was based at Wittering. When the Second War came, bomber technology had come a long way, and the 'thirties had seen the development of a defence in depth involving Anti-aircraft [AA] guns, searchlights, visual spotting, Radar, and fighters. In addition there were barrage balloons and a whole range of hopeful devices such as cables projected into the air to be suspended by parachute in order to slice off the wings of unwary bombers.

On the outbreak of War the majority of AA defences were deployed around airfields which generally had, at most, a troop of four 40mm Bofors guns. In some cases, however, the only weapons available were old WW1 vintage Lewis guns on LAA

Stanground: a British Concrete Federation hut at the Heavy AA battery site.

mounts. In January 1940, Duxford was defended by obsolete Naval 3inch guns. All these guns were manned by Territorial Army [TA] units. Searchlights were grouped in threes and positioned at about five mile intervals. The HQ of 40 AA Brigade was at Sawston Hall initially, and then at nearby Pampisford Hall. Under brigade command was 60 Searchlight Regiment with HQ at Hinxton Grange. In June 1940, searchlight sites were designated 'strongpoints' and defences were erected which included wire, trenches and a pillbox. Examples of such sites may still be identified at Quy, Ramsey, Thorney and Chatteris. By 1941 and the Baedecker Raids both Cambridge and Peterborough

42

had received modern 3.7inch HAA guns. Cambridge had a battery sited on the Newmarket Road near the airfield. In Peterborough there were gunsites at Longthorpe, now disappeared under housing, and at Stanground where the site is marked by two decaying BCF huts. Early in 1940 there had been a LAA battery at Walton, in Peterborough, made up of 20 Lewis guns. This was later replaced when the factories were given their own protection. Baker-Perkins on Westfield Road put twin Lewis guns on the tower of its factory building. These were later replaced by a 20mm Oerlikon LAA gun. Peter Brotherhoods made similar arrangements on a specially constructed mounting on the roof. Marshalls, had hoped to obtain a 40mm Bofors LAA gun but were forced to make do with two machine-guns, one mounted on the roof of the Control building, and the other mobile on the back of a truck.

Each LAA battery of 16 guns needed a complement of over 300 personnel, and ways of reducing this demand on the regular forces were sought. When, in 1941, 'Z'batteries were established in Cambridge on Walpole Road, and on Fulbridge Road in Peterborough, the Home Guard was given the task of manning them. A 'Z' battery was a collection of 64 twin projectors firing 3.25inch unrotated rockets. The idea was to create a barrage in front of approaching bombers to divert them from their targets. Later still as gun-laying radar and other technical

advances were introduced, large numbers of ATS women joined the AA brigades. Despite radar, it was still necessary to use searchlights to distinguish between genuine enemy aircraft and Duppel (the German version of Window). In 1944 when the V-weapons began to arrive, all AA resources were redeployed to the coastal strip.

Warboys: the mast of the Ground Control Interceptor radar station.

Warboys: the blockhouse of the Ground Control Interceptor radar station.

As well as for gun-laying, radar was also being developed for fighter control. Just outside Warboys is a Ground Control Interceptor [GCI] radar station which enabled pairs of fighters to be locked on to particular incoming aircraft, specifically at night. The transmitter tower, recently refurbished perhaps for the benefit of mobile 'phone users, and the control blockhouse, of 1941, both remain, surrounded by Dacoit fencing.

A further aid to air defence was the Decoy site. Most airfields were provided with a dummy site which would draw the enemy bomber away from the real target. Maxey was a decoy for Wittering, Horseheath,

45

**Maxey: the blockhouse of the bombing decoy,
a K/Q site for RAF Wittering.**

near Linton, for Duxford, and Littleport,
for Mildenhall, over the border in Suffolk.
Daylight sites, or 'K' sites had dummy
aircraft, vehicles and buildings.
Horseheath had dummy Hurricanes. Night-
time sites, or 'Q' sites, had dummy
flarepaths which were lit from a protective
bunker. These bunkers still survive at
both Maxey and Littleport, and, having
been built to standard designs, are
instantly recognisable. Civilian targets
were protected by 'SF', or Starfish sites,
often a combination of fires and lights.
Here, the site would be activated just as
the bombers arrived so that the pilots
would think that they were adding their
bombs to those first over the target.
March, one of the biggest marshalling
yards in Europe, [now Whitemoor Prison]

had both lights and fires, the lights cunningly simulating the sparks and glow from locomotives'fireboxes. Fires would be lit in braziers. Peterborough had Starfish sites at Eye, and at Stanground where the bunker still stands. Cambridge had decoy sites at Comberton [2], Fulbourn, and Babraham. Somersham, as well as being a special operations training area, was also a QL site for Wyton. Some associated structures are just visible.

Across the whole country, but particularly in the East, there was a network of visual aircraft spotting posts manned by the Royal Observer Corps [ROC]. Cambridge was the HQ of 15 Group, later redesignated

RAF Warboys: the guardroom of the post-war Bloodhound missile site.

Harston: the Royal Observer Corps underground nuclear attack monitoring post, one of several stood down in 1968; some continued in service until the end of the Cold War.

7 Group and relocated at Bedford. Sawtry, St. Ives, Ramsey, Willingham, Parson Drove, March, Soham, Harston, Castor and Whittlesey were amongst those places given ROC posts.

Both Cambridge and Peterborough experienced air-raids from early on in the War and shelters were built and rescue services provided, mainly by volunteers outside long working hours. Shelters are occasionally unearthed, as in recent building work at Parkside in Cambridge. Air-raid shelters can still be seen in the railway embankments near Westfield and

Spital Bridges in Peterborough. At Rings End, a shelter stands next to the former school-house. Personal shelters may still remain in back-gardens. At the Imperial War Museum in Duxford can be seen examples of such shelters. In Cambridge, the lily pond in front of The Fitzwilliam Museum became a static water tank for the use of the fire service, and Old Addenbrookes housed a gas decontamination unit. In Peterborough there were depots for the use of fire and rescue personnel in the St John's Street Corporation Yard, in Mountsteven Avenue, in Tennyson Road, off the Oundle Road, in the cellars of the brewery next to the Savoy Cinema, and in the old Railway Yard at Barnack. With the onset of the Cold War the ROC posts were recommissioned as an underground monitoring system in the event of nuclear attack. Despite the presence in the county of some of the key elements in a national defence strategy, there are few other signs of precaution against nuclear attack. Brooklands Avenue in Cambridge housed the Regional Seat of Government [RSG4] and the local military HQ. British Telecom Microwave towers, components of the BACKBONE Home Defence Communications system stand at Over, Morborne Hill and Wisbech. Brampton, through the'70s and '80s housed the RAF Home Defence Forces Control Centre. The depot near Caxton, now used for Go-Karting has been a Buffer Depot for the stockpiling of emergency food supplies.

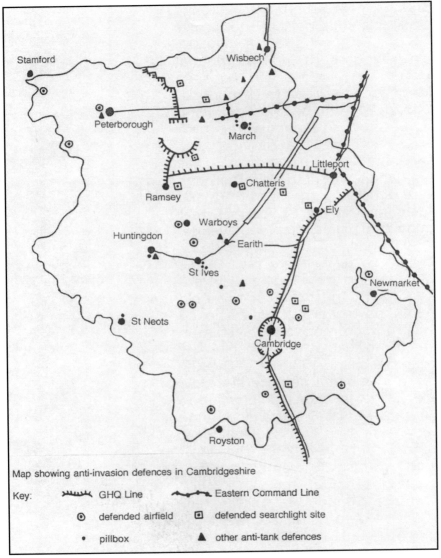

Map showing anti-invasion defences in Cambridgeshire

Key:

⌣⌣⌣⌣ GHQ Line   ◆━◆━◆ Eastern Command Line

◉ defended airfield   ▣ defended searchlight site

• pillbox   ▲ other anti-tank defences

DEFENCE AGAINST INVASION

Throughout the Great War, much of East Anglia served as a vast, armed camp attempting to meet the Western Front's insatiable need for troops. The scare literature such as Erskine Childers' "Riddle of the Sands", had alerted the prewar authorities to the dangers of a German invasion centred on the Wash, so troops were deployed appropriately. The cyclists of the Huntingdonshire Cyclists' Battalion found themselves, for instance, patrolling the coast around Spurn Head. Similarly, the gunners of the Ist Northamptonshire Battery of field artillery, recruited in Peterborough, but belonging to a unit headquartered in Hertford, in 1914 were stationed on the east coast, digging pits so that their 13pdr guns might gain sufficient elevation to engage Zeppelins. But soon these troops were off to Egypt and Palestine where, outside Gaza, they occupied a position which they christened 'Milton' to remind themselves of home and the big house on the outskirts of Peterborough. The area around Ely and Stretham contained enormous transit

camps. Artillery units were based by the grounds of Priory Hill House in St. Neots, and, when the weather was bad the guns and transport were drawn up on the hardstanding of the Market Square. Most volunteers would make their way to the county regimental depots in Northampton, Norwich or Bury, to be shipped to France as quickly as possible. Since so many of the University had gone to war, the colleges in Cambridge were empty and digs were unoccupied, much officer training took place in Cambridge to make use of so much spare capacity. Trinity College established open-air wards for soldiers to recuperate in the summer months, and, on the site of the University Library, stood the 1st. East Anglian General Hospital in prefabricated buildings. In the north of the county, Burghley House, and Milton Hall, also housed military hospitals, for soldiers wounded at the Front.

On the outbreak of the Second World War, the majority of the standing regular army was deployed either in northern France or around the Empire and, once again, home defence relied on territorials. During 1939 and 1940, the Norfolks, the Suffolks and the Cambridgeshires were all stationed in East Anglia either training or in a coast defence role. After Dunkirk there was a strong expectation of invasion. It was found out later, that Goering had set his heart on Burghley House as his British residence. Since most of the Army's transport and artillery had been left behind

on the beaches, it was impossible, in the short term at least, to plan anything other than a static defence. Ironside's strategy, then, was as follows. A coastal crust made up of coast batteries, beach obstacles, minefields, and concrete blockhouses was designed to delay enemy landings. A continuous line of anti tank obstacles was then built back from the coast. What mobile reserves there were, deployed behind this line, in order to counter-attack. This line was known as the GHQ Line and runs from the Bristol Channel, across southern England to the Medway, across the Hoo Peninsular, and so to the Thames. It then runs north up through Essex to Chelmsford, along the Cam to Cambridge, on to Ely and Littleport, and then west to Ramsey. It then goes north past Benwick, round Whittlesey, over the Nene at Dog-in a-Doublet, through Thorney and up to the Welland near Crowland. For most of its course through Cambridgeshire the Line follows waterways and is defended by pillboxes, gun emplacements and other obstacles. Cambridge was designated a 'Defended Place'which meant it was expected to hold out independently in event of attack, and the Line runs around the east of the town to create an anti-tank island. Another similar defence line starts at the coast south-east of Colchester and travels diagonally across East Anglia, eventually following the River Lark to Littleport where the two lines meet. The Eastern Command Line then continues via Downham Market towards March, meeting the Nene at Guyhirn. North of the Welland there seems to have been little construction beyond the setting of demolition charges on crossings of the Witham and Trent.

A wide variety of defensive structures may be seen along these Lines. The rivers and other waterways provide ready-made anti-tank ditches in most parts, but an artificial ditch was dug around much of Cambridge, and in other places it was necessary to dig linking sections of ditch. Crossing points were often strengthened by using anti-tank blocks or rails. On roads and railways, slots were prepared for anti-

Swaffham Bulbeck: isolated Type 22 pillbox on high ground, probably built to protect a searchlight site.

Crowtree Farm, Newborough: a Type 24 pill-box built Autumn 1940 as part of the GHQ Line.

Stone Bridge Corner, B1040: a hexagonal, shell-proof pillbox built Autumn 1940 as part of the GHQ Line.

Bodsey Bridge, Forty Foot Drain: a rectangular pillbox for three light machine-guns, built Autumn 1940 as part of the GHQ Line.

tank rails to be inserted when needed. Along the whole length of both Lines a range of pillbox types was used. These were drawn from the designs supplied by the Fortifications and Works department of the War Office, and were given Type Numbers from 22 to 28. Other designs, particularly those used on the Eastern Command Line, were locally-designed and numbered. The most common is a shellproof hexagonal structure which accommodated an infantry section with rifles and Bren light machine guns. A smaller, thinner-walled, hexagonal pillbox [Type 24] was also widely used. Particularly vulnerable points were provided with emplacements for light guns- either the

56

Euximoor House Farm, Popham's Eau: a Type 28 emplacement for 2pdr. anti tank gun built Autumn 1940 as part of the extension of the Eastern Command Line; similar emplacements stand on the GHQ Line proper elsewhere in the country.

Hobbs Lot Bridge, A605/A141: a Type 28 gun emplacement for a 2pdr. AT gun, built Autumn 1940 as part of the extension of the Eastern Command Line.

Littleport: the pedestal mounting, with its nine fixing bolts, for a 6pdr. Hotchkiss QF gun, in a Type 28 emplacement built Autumn 1940 as part of the GHQ Line.

2pounder anti-tank gun, or the 6pounder Hotchkiss Quick-Firing gun. The 2pdr. was in short supply as many had been left in France and it was essentially the same gun which was needed for tank armament at this time. The 6pdr. was a naval gun used on Edwardian Dreadnoughts, put in store,

58

Earith Bulwark: an Allan Williams turret in situ.

brought out to arm WW1 male tanks, put back into store, and then, once more, retrieved for use in another desperate situation. The emplacements, [Type 28] were simply prepared positions, and were never, fortunately, actually armed. There was no armour-piercing ammunition for the 6pdr. anyway. The two emplacements are similar, but those for the 2pdr. gun have a wider embrasure, and slots to accommodate the gun's forward-facing split trail, whilst that for the 6pdr. has a circular, steel plate with nine bolts, mounted on a concrete pedestal, centred in a narrower embrasure. Both guns had shields which, with additional sandbagging would fill the opening. The emplacements often had one chamber for the gun, and a second for Bren guns and rifles. There was also a rectangular pillbox in use which

provided three loopholes for rifles or Bren guns, and a fourth in a separate blast-wall covering the entrance at the rear. Many of these pillboxes now appear very exposed, but it must be remembered that they were integrated with other defences-trenches, wire, mines, AT obstacles, and other pillboxes with inter-locking fields of fire, most of which elements will now, of course, have disappeared. Whilst the defensive strategy was determined in the War Cabinet, the actual construction was very much a local concern. Royal Engineer officers supervised local builders sub-contracted by a Group Contractor. Hugh Cave in Thorney, and Coulson and Son in Cambridge were examples of Group Contractors. Working through the Federation of Master-builders in Tenison Road, Cambridge, the work was apportioned on a competitive tendering system but with some rationalisation. Builders were usually, for instance, awarded contracts for adjacent sites to cut down waste in transporting men and building materials There were still problems however. Some sites were inaccessible. To reach the sites for two shell-proof pillboxes and an anti-tank gun emplacement at Welches Dam on the Old Bedford River, Hugh Cave had to lay railway tracks to get the materials in. Even if the site was convenient, very often the materials were in short supply. Many of the Federation's minutes of Autumn 1940, whilst coy about recording defence sites, are quite forthright in discussing

shortages, priorities and rationing. Even though the military tried to enable economies to be effected- a weaker mix for walls unlikely to face enemy fire, [how could they tell?] and the omission of floors, for instance, the circumstances of the Fens imposed quite different demands. Drainage, or lack of it, often necessitated thick concrete rafts for the 100 ton gun-emplacements, and Drainage Boards insisted that defence works should not be allowed to interfere with flood defences. Wood was often unavailable for shuttering, so many Cambridgeshire pillboxes have permanent, brick shuttering. It would appear that the difficulties were, for the most part, overcome, as the numerous surviving structures testify to their durability nearly 60 years on. As Hugh Cave once put it, it cost more to demolish a pillbox than it had to build it originally.

Cambridge was seen as a place capable of all-round defence. An artificial anti-tank ditch was dug, largely by civilian labour, running from Babraham Road, over Worts Causeway, Queen Edith's Way, Cherry Hinton Road, Coldham's Lane, inside Marshall's Aerodrome, and across the Newmarket road to the River Cam and the railway. On the north, another AT ditch ran from the river, across Milton Road, Kings Hedges Road, Arbury Road and Histon Road, finishing short of the Huntingdon road. On the west there was only a short length of ditch extending about 500yards [450m] north and south

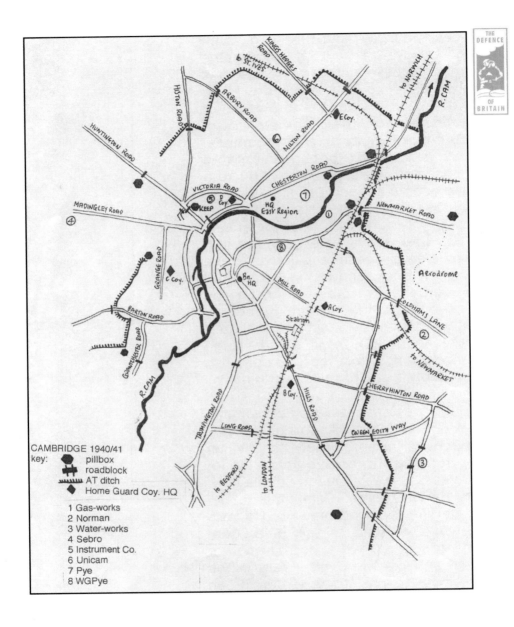

CAMBRIDGE 1940/41
key:
- pillbox
- roadblock
- AT ditch
- Home Guard Coy. HQ

1 Gas-works
2 Norman
3 Water-works
4 Sebro
5 Instrument Co.
6 Unicam
7 Pye
8 WGPye

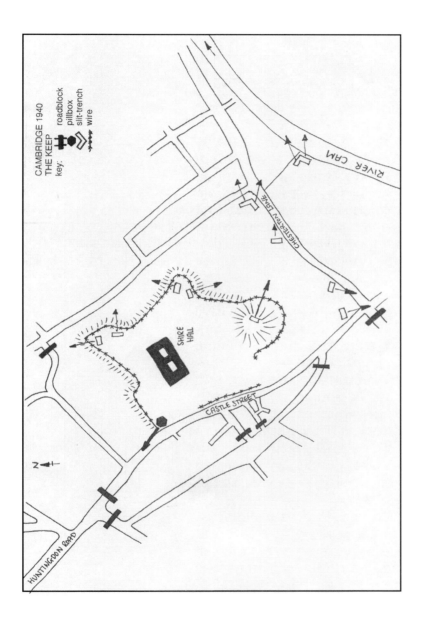

CAMBRIDGE 1940
THE KEEP
key:
roadblock
pillbox
slit-trench
wire

RIVER CAM

CHESTERTON LANE

SHIRE HALL

CASTLE STREET

HUNTINGDON ROAD

N

THE
DEFENCE
OF
BRITAIN

of Barton Road. Virtually every road into Cambridge was protected by a roadblock, consisting of steel rails to be inserted into prepared slots across the width of the road on receipt of a written order. On the east side of town two inner defence lines were defined. One followed the railway between the Gas Works and the Station, then ran west along Brooklands Avenue to the Cam. The other followed the old Civil War defence line down East Road and Gonville Place and along Lensfield Road. Both inner lines converged on the river at Coe Fen. The final point of resistance was the 'Keep'- quite literally, the Castle Hill/Shire Hall complex, a site fortified in Roman, Norman, mediaeval, and Civil War times. It was now defended with roadblocks, slit trenches, and a pillbox facing up the Huntingdon road. Other pillboxes were built around the town and some still stand, including a fine anti-tank gun emplacement near the Football Ground. The history of the Cambridgeshire Home Guard relates how one platoon put 1000yards [915m] of double apron barbed wire around their pillboxes. As well as the roadblocks, the men of 'G' Company- the LNER railwaymen, would erect railblocks, twelve in all, to prevent attacking forces from using the railway tracks as a means of by-passing road obstructions. The overall defence of Cambridge was the responsibility of 5 Battalion of the Cambridgeshire Home Guard, whose five rifle companies [A-E] were each allocated a segment of the town to defend. The Battalion HQ was

at the Music School in Downing Place. Detached platoons were maintained at many of the town's more vulnerable sites, such as Norman's Cement Works, Pye's works, the Instrument Company, Sebro and Unicam. The platoon at Pye's, off the Chesterton road, was further charged with defending St. Regis House in Montague Road, the Eastern Regional military HQ. Marshall's Aerodrome was defended by 50 men of an RAF Training Wing. Three permanent traffic checkpoints at Milton Road, Barnwell Bridge, and Hills Road Bridge were maintained by civil and military police with support from 6 NCOs and 24 men drawn from E, A, and B Companies. Standing orders, as with all closures and demolitions, was to allow as much friendly traffic through as possible before taking emergency action. Two tasks were envisaged for these local, and non-regular, forces. In the event of an invasion on the east coast, to keep open routes for reinforcements by delaying the enemy's advance, and defending the town to the last. In the event of a small-scale airborne raid, to attack and destroy enemy infantry whilst using the roadblocks to deny enemy transport opportunity to manoeuvre. By 1941 the Cambridge Defence Plan was to show in comprehensive detail that with the arsenal of weapons then available, and with the two University battalions-one of which as an officer training unit was equipped with armour and artillery as a mobile strike force, these tasks might have been realistic expectations, but in

1940 it was a tall order. In an anthology of Home Guard reminiscences, a home guardsman in Grantchester explained how he and the Classics professor were given the Stokes Mortar and told to stop the THIRD panzer as it crossed the Mill Bridge. Their colleagues had worked it all out! The first tank would be allowed to go through and round two sharp bends. A mine in the middle of the road would stop it, and hidden home guards would haul a mine across behind it. It would be set alight by Molotov cocktails. The same thing would happen to the second tank on the first bend; but the third tank would be despatched with the Stokes Mortar, thus blocking the bridge to further enemy advance. Allan Lawrie, who described this plan, refers to the Stokes Mortar as a sort of metal drainpipe, but does not say whether the mines were real or not. Tom Wintringham, who commanded part of the International Brigade in Spain, and later trained home guards, describes some of the tricks of street-fighting. Upturned soup-plates in the road simulating mines could be just as effective as real ones in forcing tanks to stop, and thus to become vulnerable to sticky bombs and the like. The important thing was to make the enemy tank-commander believe there was a mine in front of his tank. Also in Wintringham's book are instructions for turning houses, especially those overlooking roadblocks, into strongpoints, even in tranquil villages like Grantchester.

We have met the Stokes Mortar above.

Earith Bulwark: a Spigot Mortar pedestal, originally standing in a pit.

Another home guard weapon in plentiful supply was the Spigot Mortar or Blacker Bombard. This fired a 14 or 20 pound bomb over ranges of a few hundred yards. It was fired from a prepared position which consisted of a thimble-shaped concrete pedestal about three feet [1 m] high in a brick-lined pit with alcoves for storing the bombs. Embedded in the top of the pedestal was a stainless steel pintle on which was set the mortar. Many of these remain in Cambridgeshire. There was also a portable field mounting with spade feet. In 1941 the 5 Bn. Home Guard had 31 Northover Projectors, which fired glass, self-igniting phosphorus bombs, and 92 Spigot Mortars for the defence of Cambridge. Along with a Smith Gun whose dustbinlid-like shield doubled as a

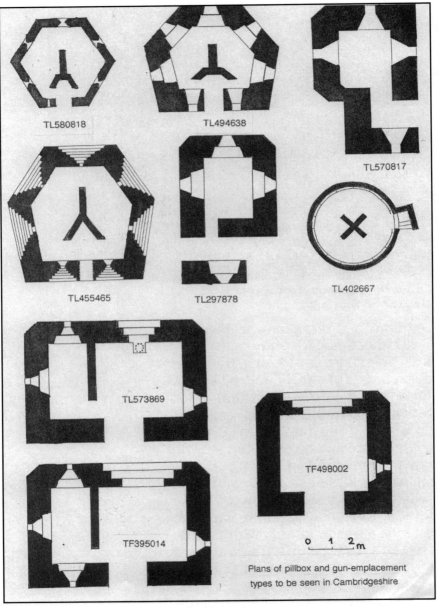

TL580818

TL494638

TL570817

TL455465

TL297878

TL402667

TL573869

TF498002

TF395014

0 1 2 m

Plans of pillbox and gun-emplacement
types to be seen in Cambridgeshire

THE
DEFENCE
OF
BRITAIN

Newborough: a Home Guard store/shelter, one of several in the County.

wheel, these weapons may be seen at Duxford Museum.

Large parts of the GHQ Line defences survive. A gun emplacement at Whittlesford Mill, and two pillboxes, at Ickleton, and Great Shelford represent the only standing remains south of Cambridge, but this would seem to confirm that not all those planned, were actually built. Around Cambridge itself there are five pillboxes and a gun emplacement. Eight pillboxes stand between Cambridge and Ely, and the Ely-Queen Adelaide-Prickwillow-Littleport position accounts for five gun emplacements, and nine assorted pillboxes. Beyond Littleport northwards are two more pillboxes before the Norfolk border is reached at Brandon Creek. The

69

Line westwards from Littleport can be seen where a gun emplacement and three pillboxes stand at Pymore, and on the other side of the Bedford Rivers where there are two gun emplacements and five pillboxes up to the end of this part of the Line in Ramsey. A crescent of defences runs from above Benwick to Floods Ferry and consists of a gun emplacement and nine pillboxes. There is an uncompleted stretch of Line between Benwick and Lattersey Hill, where bridges, such as Angle Bridge, were set for demolition, but pillboxes do not reappear until east of Whittlesey, which is ringed by a string of thirteen extending to the Nene, and includes one gun emplacement. Between

Elm: two anti-tank rails; another stands on the other side of the road, and slots in the road surface would have taken others in an emergency.

Speechley's Drove, Newborough: an anti-tank block next to a bridge over the anti-tank ditch of the GHQ Line; a chamber contained explosives to blow the bridge.

the river-crossing at Dog-in-a-Doublet and Thorney there are ten pillboxes, and from there to the end of this section of the Line at the Welland, there is one gun emplacement, and twenty pillboxes. The Eastern Command Line which continued from Brandon Creek to Downham Market, before turning west, re-enters Cambridgeshire near Three Holes. Two gun emplacements and nine pillboxes can be found between here and Guyhirn. The road and railway crossings at Guyhirn are defended by two square pillboxes, three spigot mortar pedestals, and, formerly, by AT rails in concrete sockets on the railway line.

RAF Little Staughton: the Battle HQ, to the standard 11008/41 design.

RAF Waterbeach: the Battle HQ, a non-standard design with hexagonal cupola on a sunken rectangular shelter.

Particularly in view of possible airborne attacks, airfields needed their own defences.in the event of a landing by either parachutists or glider-borne troops, the airfield's defence would have been directed from the Battle HQ. This was a sunken, concrete control room with telephone exchange, a room for runners, and so on, and at one end, an all-round observation slit under a thick, concrete cupola, where the commander of the airfield's defence force could see what was going on. This usually overlooked the landing area, as did some of the pillboxes or other strongpoints. There was a standard design for the Battle HQ- 11008/41. Examples of the standard design can be seen at Little Staughton and Warboys. A unique design with a

RAF Waterbeach: a semi-sunken pillbox with tunnel entrance and pistol-loop above, on the edge of the flying area.

RAF Duxford: a hexagonal machine-gun post, with sunken entrance.

RAF Snailwell, Newmarket: a hexagonal pill-box strengthened up to loophole height at a later date.

74

RAF Wyton: a square pillbox with half-height blastwall.

hexagonal cupola on top of a bomb shelter stands beside the Watch Office at Waterbeach. The Air Ministry provided its own pillbox designs which differed from those of the War Office. There were straightforward square and hexagonal types, but there was also an odd circular model, the manufacturers being the FCConstruction Co. Ltd. A parasol roof is supported on a cruciform wall which stands in a sunken, circular pit. The brick sides of the pit rise almost to meet the overhanging roof thus creating an all-round field of fire. A continuous rail just below parapet level, carries mounts for two machine-guns. The type is often referred to as the Oakington pillbox, and it may have originated there, where seven still

RAF Oakington: one of the several FCConstruction pillboxes still standing round the perimeter of the airfield.

stand, but the Company's original plan is for the eight they built at Burnaston in Derbyshire, now all under the Toyota plant. As well as those at Oakington, there are FCConstruction pillboxes at Warboys and Caxton Gibbet. One of the Air Ministry's directives was that pillboxes should have their walls thickened to shellproof standard and at Snailwell there are three hexagonal pillboxes where this improvement has been implemented. Many airfield pillboxes had Turnbull mounts fitted to their loopholes so that light machine-guns could be used more effectively. A fine example of an attempt to improve the mobility of the airfield's defenders is the conversion into armoured cars at Marshall' Aerodrome of

76

two Austin Twelve cars, by the addition of sheets of boiler-plate, and slight modifications to the springs. Usually army detachments were responsible for airfield defence, until, in 1942, the RAF Regiment was formed specifically for that purpose. Many of these airfield defences have disappeared. Peterborough, for instance, is known to have had a Battle HQ, and two Allan-Williams turrets, small, steel, revolving cupolas, entered through a ground-level hatch, and with room for two men and mountings for an anti-aircraft light machine-gun, and another to counter ground attack. Here, only a conventional pillbox survives.

Huntingdon was an anti-tank island, like Cambridge, but on a smaller scale. A

St Marys Street, Huntingdon: the location of the Drill Hall and Home Guard HQ.

pillbox still stands covering the bridge at Godmanchester, and others ran along the railway line toward St. Ives. The Iron Bridge had four small sentry posts at the level of the railway line, and below there, in St. Peters Road , anti-tank blocks, a spigot mortar pedestal, a pillbox, and a loopholed wall all stood until the recent redevelopment of the site. From this strongpoint a ditch with wire entanglements ran down the line of the Ring Road to the river, where there were more anti-tank blocks. Finally, the western approach was sealed by a roadblock covered by a pillbox at Nun's Bridge on the Brampton road near Hinchingbrooke House. The local Home Guard HQ was at the Drill Hall in St. Mary's Street, with a rifle range nearby behind Castle Hills House. The Lewis-gun range was further away, near Grafham.

Other crossings of the Ouse were also defended. At St. Ives pillboxes survive near the old parish church, a rectangular one enfilading a stretch of river upstream from the bridge, and two hexagonal ones stand alongside the railway just south of the station. At St. Neots a hexagonal pillbox stands at the town end of the common. At Earith, where the Old and New Bedford Rivers head north from the Great Ouse, the defences are centred on the old Cromwellian fort. An Allan-Williams Turret stands on the south-east bastion, and two spigot mortar pedestals command the approaches. In 1940, and

78

**Willow Hall, Eye: the alleged bridgehead HQ
of a German airborn invasion.**

again after the fall of Crete, there were fears of a landing from the air. Obstacles were positioned in likely landing fields, and in some places trenches were dug to impede gliders. These measures were taken in St. Ives when farm-labourers, shopkeepers, schoolboys and cadets were mobilised on Sundays and Thursday afternoons, [early-closing] to dig anti-glider ditches in 100 yard squares, in the water-meadows of Hemingford Grey. Below Houghton, at Hemingford Abbots, the alternative of poles holding taut wires was chosen. There is a tradition that Willow Hall, south of the A47 between Eye and Thorney, was earmarked for the HQ of German airborne troops which would land by glider on the exceptionally flat and obstacle-free fields which stretched for nearly a mile in each direction behind the Hall. Pre-War reconnaissance would have identified such locations from the planes of Lufthansa, or the bicycles of the Hitler Youth.

Peterborough was important as both a nodal point in terms of communications, and as an industrial centre. The river crossing of the Nene was defended by a pillbox and anti-tank blocks, one of which remains near Town Bridge, and the northern approaches were defended at the point where the Wisbech railway line crossed Lincoln Road. On the west the airfield complex and Baker Perkins with its own Home Guard detachment and AA guns, guarded the town and railway. The whole of the city was ringed by road-blocks, and the keep was located in the Power Station near the bridges over the Nene. The Home Guard commander of the Keep was also manager of the Power Station and managed to electrify the perimeter wire. Only after the local cat population fell below replacement level was this particular defensive strategy abandoned. The eastern side was protected by the GHQ Line coming up from Whittlesey and through Thorney to Newborough and the Welland. The 1st [City of Peterborough] Battalion of the Northamptonshire Home Guard was soon supplemented by the 2nd[Soke of Peterborough] Battalion. Whilst the 1st

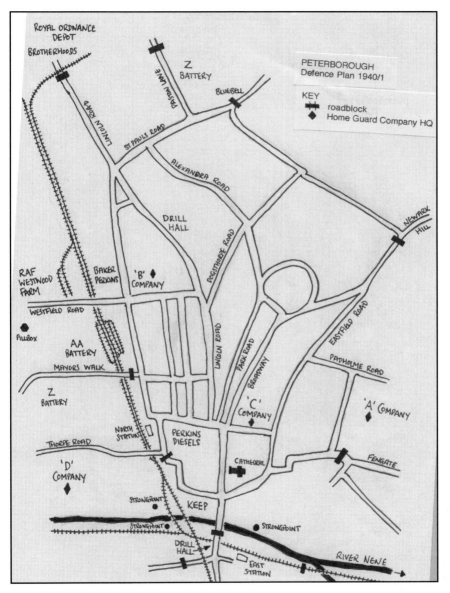

PETERBOROUGH
Defence Plan 1940/1

KEY
⊨ roadblock
◆ Home Guard Company HQ

THE
DEFENCE
OF
BRITAIN

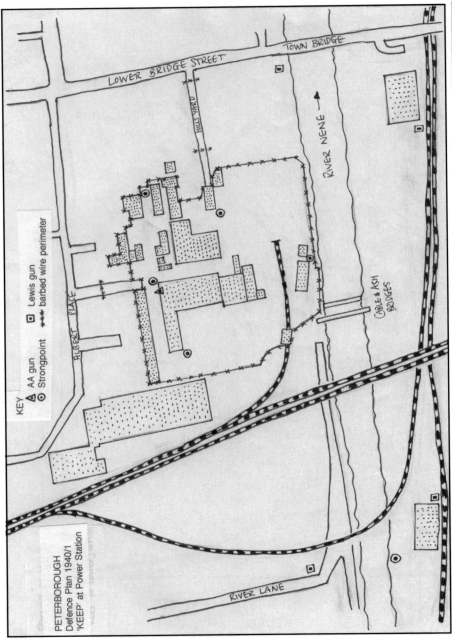

KEY

△ AA gun
◎ Strongpoint
▣ Lewis gun
✕✕✕ barbed wire perimeter

PETERBOROUGH
Defence Plan 1940/1
'KEEP' at Power Station

THE
DEFENCE
OF
BRITAIN

Bn. had responsibility for the city- from Thorpe Hall north to Paston, and then back down to the river, the 2nd Bn.with its HQ at the Cock Inn, Werrington, and maintaining companies at Castor, Werrington, and Dogsthorpe, was charged with safeguarding vulnerable points such as the Great North Road viaduct at Wansford, and the Ordnance Depot at Walton. The whole of the County was well-served by the Home Guard. Besides the three battalions in Cambridge itself, there were four additional battalions in the surrounding villages. The Isle of Ely had raised a Territorial Army battalion which subsequently became the 2nd Cambridgeshires and arrived in Singapore during the collapse. However, two Home Guard battalions were still raised, centred on Ely, Chatteris, and March. One unit of the Home Guard little written about until recently was the British Resistance Organisation, small cells of men who knew the land and could live off it. In the event of invasion they would go underground and emerge only to carry out acts of sabotage and guerilla warfare. Many of their hides still exist and there was certainly a patrol with a base in Elm. These hides were built to a standard pattern, with two entrances, and were fully-equipped with stocks of food, weapons, ammunition, and explosives.

One way around the lack of mobility, in the early days, was the use of armoured trains on the remote Feniand lines around

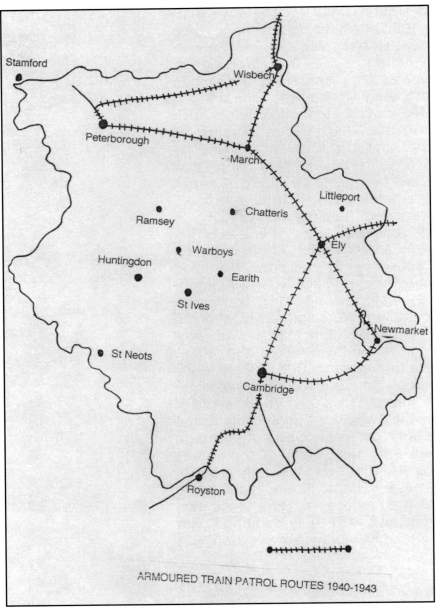

Stamford

Wisbech

Peterborough

March

Littleport

Chatteris

Ramsey

Warboys

Huntingdon

Earith

St Ives

Ely

Newmarket

St Neots

Cambridge

Royston

ARMOURED TRAIN PATROL ROUTES 1940-1943

the Wash. Each train comprised a 2-4-2 tank engine, [LNER F4], chosen for its suitability by Sir Nigel Gresley, better-known for his achievements with slightly quicker locomotives, and two each of two LMS wagons- a three-plank drop-side, and a 24foot [7.4m] coal-wagon.A fighting truck at each end of the train carried a Hotchkiss 6pounder QF gun, a Boys anti-tank rifle, and two bren-guns on AA mountings. The locomotive and tender were placed centrally, and the three-plank truck carrying stores was positioned either side of the loco. Boiler-plate was used to armour the locomotive, tender, and fighting trucks. The patrols carried out by these trains varied throughout the War. In 1941, Train 'M' was based in Spalding and operated around Peterborough, March and the Wash generally. Train 'G' patrolled north of a line from Cambridge to Thetford. Train 'A' spent a period of time covering the Hitchin-Cambridge-Bedford triangle, and, late in 1941, No1 Group, with five trains under command, was based in Cambridge.

_I_NDUSTRY AND AGRICULTURE

The Great War posed a problem for the agricultural community. The armies on the Western Front needed replenishing with manpower to make good the enormous losses, but they also needed feeding, as did the munitions workers in the cities. Charles Adeane of Babraham Hall was, in 1914, Lord Lieutenant of Cambridgeshire, Commandant of the Cambridgeshire Volunteers, and President of the Royal Agricultural Society of England. His wife, Madeline, was President of the ladies' Recruitment Committee for Cambridge-shire. All the young men of Babraham volunteered for the Army, and other sorties were equally successful- on 5 September 1914, for instance, Ely was visited and 26 men recruited. Adeane saw as his role the defence of the farmers, but also promoted new ideas, especially the employment of women as agricultural workers. By 1916 he employed 18 women on the Babraham Estate.

On the industrial front, Sages, the aircraft factory in Peterborough, pioneered the production and successful operation of a rearward-firing machine-gun in fighter aircraft. They also received contracts from the Admiralty to build Short 184 seaplanes in 1915, completing 82 in all. Marshalls, in Cambridge, repaired and serviced Rolls Royce armoured cars and military ambulances, in their Jesus Lane garage.

The second war made even greater demands on labour. The Defence of the Realm Act gave the Minister of Food Production complete control over agriculture through County Agriculture Committees who were empowered. to take possession of under- achieving farms. At the same time, prices were guaranteed. All available personnel were drafted onto the land; girls of the Women's Land Army, Italian prisoners of war and evacuees from the East End of London. Food had to be grown, harvested, processed, stored and distributed. The enormous grain silos in Dogsthorpe built for the Ministry of Food [Cereal Products Division] in 1943, like the Government Cold Store near Botolph Bridge, were provided with private railway sidings.

On the outbreak of war, targets in Cambridge quickly identified themselves and took the appropriate air-raid precautions. These firms included Unicam, manufacturing optical equipment for guns and submarines; Pyes, making radio equipment- the Cambridge Instrument

Company making compasses etc. for the Admiralty; Sebro with its aircraft parts operation; and Marshalls who, as well as training pilots, employed up to 3000 workers repairing, maintaining, re-building, re-fitting, and converting a vast range of aircraft and gliders for the Ministry of Aircraft Production.

Peterborough's engineering industry converted immediately to war production. At Westwood Works, Baker Perkins built Twin-6 pounder Coast Defence guns, 6 pounder AT guns, 25 pounder, 4.5 and 5.5inch medium guns, and, later on, 17 pounder AT guns. Turrets, fitted with 17 or 25 pounder guns were developed for D- Day landing craft. Often parts had to be improvised, and new ones developed

Walton, Peterborough: the former Royal Army Ordnance Corps depot.

to be supplied to other weapons factories. Equally vital were the mobile bakeries used abroad by the services, and at home by the bombed-out. Peter Brotherhoods, over the railway from Westwood, made torpedoes for the Navy. These were taken to be stored at the Royal Navy Armaments Depot in a disused brick-pit in Warboys. Next door to Brotherhoods was the Royal Army Ordnance Depot at Walton. South of the river, BTH in Woodston made parts for Wellington bombers, Mitchell Engineering was a contractor for the LNER, and Newalls were important enough to warrant a private siding. Out at Nassington the ironstone quarries helped compensate for the shortfall in imported ore. London Brick provided the materials for many of the

Fridaybridge Prisoner-of-war Camp, now an international farm hostel.

new building demanded by a nation at war, and made available one of their worked-out pits as a store for Aviation Fuel, served by a private branch-line.

PRISONER-OF-WAR CAMPS
In the Great War there were POW camps at:

Littleport	Cambridge, Newmarket Road	Linton
Chesterton	Cambridge Military Hospital	Upware
Glatton	Kimbolton Castle Stables	St Neots
Wennington	Papworth St Agnes	Brampton
Huntingdon	Gamlingay, Little Gransden	Caxton
Meldreth	Arrington, Hardwick Arms	

In the Second World War camps were established at:

Milton Road, Histon [No 1025]
Trumpington [Nos 45 and 180]
Friday Bridge near Wisbech [No 90]
West Fen Militia camp, Ely [No 130]
Newmarket [Group Pioneer Corps HQ]

Fletton: what appears to be an engine room at this former POW camp.

Other camps are known to have been at Fletton, Peterborough, where some buildings apparently remain; at Orton Hall, and at Thorney. Many POWs were billeted on individual farms to work as labourers.

Farm Hall, Godmanchester: the location of Operation Epsilon, the de-briefing of the German Atomic scientists, Summer 1945.

At the end of the war in Europe it was essential to ensure that word of developments in atomic weaponry achieved by German scientists should not leak out prior to the dropping of an 'A' bomb on Japan. At the same time there was curiosity as to whether those scientists working for a NAZI regime had soft-pedalled their work in the interests of humanity. Early in July 1945, 10 German atomic scientists were flown into Tempsford, and thence by truck to Farm Hall, a large 18th Century house in Godmanchester, owned by the British Secret Service. They were paroled in writing not to leave the Hall's grounds but otherwise left to their own devices whilst all their conversations were recorded and transcribed. The main object of their being kept incommunicado until the Hiroshima bomb on 8 August, was achieved, but close scrutiny of their conversations revealed some as fervent Nazis, and no evidence that they had done anything other than their utmost to produce a German atomic bomb. On 3 January 1946 they were returned to Germany where several resumed their academic careers.

CONCLUSION

The majority of sites mentioned in this book are visible from public rights-of-way but many are on private land and visitors should take every precaution to avoid trespass. Most landowners are very pleased to grant access on request, and a letter written in advance of any visit, invariably makes them more amenable. Some of the structures described here are on Ministry of Defence land and it is particularly important to obtain prior permission from the base commander or other relevant authority. Un-notified visits, especially where photography is involved, may attract un-looked for attention from security staff. Many of the structures concerned were built for short-term use. The process of abandonment, partial demolition, natural decay, and vandalism both official and unofficial, may have rendered them dangerous. TAKE CARE BUT ENJOY YOUR EXPLORATIONS — and please don't forget to record your observations for posterity. Often, you could be the last person to visit a particular site, before it falls down, or, even as a perfectly viable building, is demolished.

BIBLIOGRAPHY

Baker Perkins Ltd., Wartime at Baker Perkins Ltd, Peterborough, no date.

Bowyer, Michael JF; Action Stations 1: Military Airfields of East Anglia, 2nd edn, PSI, Sparkford, 2001.

Bowyer, Michael JF, Action Stations 6: Military Airfields of the Cotswolds and the Central Midlands, PSL,Sparkford, 1983 and 1990.

British Legion, Book of Brampton, Ellington, Easton, & Spaidwick, 1948 and 1987

Cambridge Defence Plan, 1941

Cambridgeshire & Isle of Ely TA Association, We Also Served, The Story of the Home Guard in Cambridgeshire and the Isle of Ely 1940-1943, Heffers, Cambridge, 1944

Francis, Paul; Control Towers, Airfield Research Publishing, Ware, 1993

Francis, Paul; British Military Airfield Architecture, PSL, Sparkford, 1996

Frank, Sir Charles [intro], Operation Epsilon, The Farm Hall Transcripts, Institute of Physics Publishing, 1993

Gibson, Michael, L; Aviation in Northamptonshire, Northants Libraries, 1982

Holloway, B. G. & Banks, H.; The Northamptonshire Home Guard, NHG, 1949

Innes, G. B., British Airfield Buildings of the Second World War, Midland, Earl Shilton, 1995

Innes, G. B., British Airfield Buildings of the Second World War, Midland, Volume 2, Earl Shilton, 2000

Longmate, N.; The Real Dad's Army, Arrow, London, 1974

Lowry, S [ed]; Twentieth Century Defences in Britain, Council for British Archaeology, 1995

MARSHALL of CAMBRIDGE [Engineering Ltd.]. Making its Contribution to the Battle of Britain, Cambridge, 1990

Ministry of Information, Roof Over Britain: AA Defences 1939-42, HMSO, London, 1943

Pile, Gen Sir F, Ack-Ack, Harrap, London, 1949

Shaw, Frank & Joan; We Remember the Home Guard, Hinckley, 1990

Slater, Hugh, Home Guard for Victory, Gollancz, London, 1941

Smith, Bridget; Digging Ditches on Hemingford Grey Meadow, Jnl of the Hunts Local History Soc. Vol3 No5, 1996

Waszak, Peter, Peterborough Wartime Private Sidings, unpublished notes, 1997

Wills, Henry, Pillboxes, Leo Cooper/Seeker&Warburg, London, 1985

Wintringham, Tom, New Ways of War, Penguin, London, 1940

GAZETTEER

AIRFIELDS

This is a list of examples, not a definitive inventory.

TL295795	Alconbury	WW2,bomber satellite; US8AAF-,USAF - present
TL330460	Bassingbourn	WW2,bomber, US8AAF; Army recruit training
TL540595	Bottisham	WW2,bomber-training; US8AAF; agriculture
TL340590	Bourn	WW2,bombers; light industry and agriculture
TL485585	Cambridge	training, maintenance, repair-, Marshalls airport
TL630425	Castle Camps	WW2,fighters-, light industry and agriculture
TL300653	Caxton Gibbet	WW2,training; agriculture
TL460460	Duxford	WW1 , WW2, fighters, US8AAF; Imp. War Museum
TL415440	Fowlmere	WW1-, WW2, fighters, US8AAF; agriculture
TL185870	Glatton[Conington]	WW2, bombers, US8AAF, Peterborough Airport
TL293555	Gransden Lodge	WW2,bombers, experimental, agriculture
TL238645	Graveley	WW2, bomber, agriculture
TL105695	Kimbolton	WW2, bomber, US8AAF-, agriculture, retail
TL120615	Little Staughton	WW2,bombers/ repair; industrial estate
TL385545	Lords Bridge	WW2, landing ground/ bomb store, Observatory
TL449795	Mepal	WW2,bomber; post-War THOR; agriculture
TL008770	Molesworth	WW2,bomber, USSAAF, post-War CRUISE,USAF
TL409655	Oakington	WW2,bomber., Home Office Use
TF165002	Peterborough	WW2,training, housing and industrial use
TL095960	Sibson	WW2,training; Parachute Centre, private flying
TL650665	Snailwell	WW2, army co-operation; agriculture and A14
TL350770	Somersham	WW2,special duties training/ Q site-, agriculture
TL302420	Steeple Marden	WW2, US8AAF fighter:bombers/photo; agriculture
TL270845	Upwood	WW1;WW2,bomber; USAF Clinic, agriculture
TL290795	Warboys	WW2, bomber pathfinder, post-War SAM-, storage
TL495665	Waterbeach	WW2,bomber, RE Airfield Construction Unit
TL520780	Witchford	WW2,bomber; industrial estate and agriculture
TF045025	Wittering	WW1;WW2, fighter; operational fighter station
TL645510	Wratting Common	WW2, bomber;DP Camp, agriculture
TL285741	Wyton	WW1;WW2, bomber, pathfinder/recce, RAF logistics

AIRFIELD BUILDINGS

TL342452	Bassingbourn	Gymnasium/Church-temporary brick [14604/40]
TL548601	Bottisham	Squadron Office- temporary brick
TL490592	Cambridge	Main Stores- permanent brick
TL490592	Cambridge	Motor Transport section- permanent brick
TL619421	Castle Camps	Officers' Mess- temporary brick

TL613420	Castle Camps	Dining Room & Institute [WAAF]- Nissen
TL302606	Caxton Gibbet	Picket Post- temporary brick
TL458462	Duxford	Guardroom- Expansion Period
TL454460	Duxford	Sickbay/Decontamination - Expansion Period
TL456464	Duxford	Gymnasium/Cinema- temporary brick
TL460462	Duxford	WW1 barrack blocks
TL549820	RAF Hospital, Ely	Water Tower- Expansion Period
TL549820	RAF Hospital, Ely	Motor Transport section - Expansion Period
TL170859	Glatton	Water Tower - steel
TLI80160	Glatton	Stand-by-set house - permanent brick
TL282554	Gransden Lodge	Operations Block - temporary brick
TL121616	Little Staughton	Fire Tender Shelter - Nissen
TL121616	Little Staughton	Night Flying Equipment Store- temporary brick
TLI22616	Little Staughton	Floodlight Tractor & Trailer Shed- temporary brick
TL123615	Little Staughton	Main Workshops- Romney Huts
TL391540	Lords Bridge	Fire Tender Shed- permanent brick
TL406664	Oakington	Station HQ- Expansion Period
TL406664	Oakington	Parachute Store- Expansion Period
TL406664	Oakington	Armoury- Expansion Period
TL404666	Oakington	Officers' Mess- Expansion Period [204/35]
TL404663	Oakington	Small-arms Range- permanent brick
TL410670	Oakington	Stand-by Set House- Expansion Period
TL175998	Peterborough	Officers Mess- Expansion Period [7035/30]
TL175998	Peterborough	Batmen's Quarters- MOWP Standard Hut
TL178999	Peterborough	Sergeants' Mess- Expansion Period[325/30]
TL178999	Peterborough	Railway platform- permanent brick
TL300796	Warboys	Air-raid shelter- permanent brick
TL294786	Warboys	Guardroom- permanent brick
TL299784	Warboys	Static Water Tank- steel
TL492664	Waterbeach	Free Gunnery Turret Trainer- temporary brick
TL493665	Waterbeach	Synthetic Navigation Classroom- temporary brick
TL493665	Waterbeach	Main Stores- Expansion Period
TL283743	Wyton	Parachute Drying Tower- Expansion Period
TL284742	Wyton	Dome Trainer- temporary brick

ANTI-AIRCRAFT SITES

TL475567	Walpole Rd.,Cambridge	former site of Z gun battery
TL4959-	Newmarket Rd., Cambridge	former site of 3.7in. HAA battery
TL523614	Quy Common,	searchlight site, pillbox remains
TL573614	Swaffham Bulbeck	searchlight site, pillbox remains
TL504465	Hinxton Grange	S'light Regt. HQ, pillbox remains
TL509484	Pampisford Hall HQ,	40 AA Brigade
TL294859	Ramsey	searchlight site, pillbox remains
TL405863	Chatteris	searchlight site, pillbox remains
TL223957	Stanground	3.7in. HAA battery, huts remain

TL174992	Longthorpe	former site of 3.7in. HAA battery
TF1801	Fulbridge Rd., Peterborough	former site of Z gun battery
TF294058	Elder House Farm, Thorney	searchlight site, pillbox remains

ANTI-TANK OBSTACLES

TF474075	Elm	3 anti-tank rails
TF218061	Newborough	1 anti-tank block with demolition-charge chamber
TF251055	Cats Water	2 anti-tank blocks beside pillbox, B1443
TF244056-248063	Slipe Farm	length of anti-tank ditch
TL192981	Peterborough	1 anti-tank block

BATTLE HEADQUARTERS

TL1 07621	Little Staughton	standard pattern 11008/41
TL299796	Warboys	standard pattern 11008/41
TL491667	Waterbeach	non-standard design, hexagonal cupola

BOMBING DECOYS

TL587482	Horseheath	QK decoy for Duxford
TL566730	Soham	Q decoy for Waterbeach
TL527545	Fulbourn	temporary Starfish for Cambridge
TL345760	Somersham	Q decoy for Wyton- some ruins discernible
TL584852	Littleport	Q decoy for Mildenhall, blockhouse remains
TL233958	Stanground	permanent QF Starfish for P'boro - blockhouse
TF452011	Coldham	QL/QF decoy for March railway yards
TF140095	Maxey	Q decoy for Wittering

CONTROL TOWERS

TL337458	Bassingbourn	Type 207/36, watch office + tower-"fort' type
TL490592	Cambridge	Civil Aerodrome control building, 1937
TL461461	Duxford	Type 343/43 for all Commands
TL284553	Gransden Lodge	Type 13726/41 for Bomber satellite stations
TL121617	Little Staughton	Type 13726/41 for Bomber satellite stations
TL491666	Waterbeach	Type 5845/39, watch office + met. section-"villa"
TF050030	Wittering	Type 2072/26 replaced by Type V Bomber/1955
TL282744	Wyton	Type 2328/39, watch office + met. section- "villa"

HANGARS

TL3345	Bassingbourn	3x 'C' Type
TL4859	Cambridge	1937 Civil type. Bl, T2, Blisters, 'A' Frame Sheds
TL4546	Duxford	WW1 Coupled GS Sheds, WW2 coupled T2s
TL4144	Fowlmere	T2 reclad
TL1261	Little Staughton	2x T2s and 2x Robins

TL6063	Newmarket	2x Bls
TL4065/6	Oakington	2x'J'Type, 2x T2s, lx Bl
TL0996	Sibson	l x TI, Beliman [from Peterborough post-War]
TL9783	Upwood	4x'C'Type
TL4966	Waterbeach	2x'J'Type, 1 x Tl, 2x T2, 1 x Bl
TF0503	Wittering	post-War Gaydon type, 2x'C'Type
TL6350	Wratting Common	2x T2s, 1 x Bl
TL2874	Wyton	4x 'C' Type, 1 short T2 [for Mosquitoes]

HEADQUARTERS

TL208710	Brampton Grange	RAF 7 Group, later US 8th Army Air Force
TL210700	Brampton Park	l st Air Division, US 8th Army Air Force
TL241715	Castle Hills House	RAF'Pathfinder'Force
TL487491	Sawston Hall	US 66th Fighter Wing
TF080042	Walcot Hall	US 67th Fighter Wing
TF248016	Willow Hall	reputed potential German airborne forces

HOME GUARD STORES/SHELTERS

TF205061	Newborough
TL265963	B1040 south of Whittlesey
TL576817	B1382 between Prickwillow and Queen Adelaide
TL399681	B1050 by level crossing north of Longstanton

PILLBOXES AND GUN EMPLACEMENTS

TF202090	River Welland	shell-proof, hexagonal pillbox built into river-bank
TF221079	Speechley's Drove	shellproof, hexagonal pillbox
TF215062	Crowtree Farm	Type 24 pillbox
TF251055	Cats Water	rectangular pillbox with rear, looped blastwall
TF279050	Bukehorn Road	Type 28 emplacement [2pdr AT gun]
TF277009	Stone Br. Corner	shellproof, hexagonal pillbox
TF275002	Teakettle Hall Fm.	shellproof, hexagonal pillbox
TF399024	Guyhirn	2 square pillboxes on bridge astride railway
TF395014	A605/A1 41	Type 28 emplacement [2pdr AT gun + bren]
TF498002	Euximoor House	Type 28 emplacement [2pdr AT gun]
TL274994	Dog-in-a-Doublet	brick, hexagonal pillbox built by County Council
TL249971	Kings Dyke	Type 28 emplacement [6pdr OF gun+ bren]
TL343909	Benwick	shellproof, hexagonal pillbox
TL356916	Copalder Corner	Type 28 emplacement [6pdr OF gun + bren]
TL297878	Bodsey Bridge	rectangular pillbox with rear, looped blastwall
TL393879	A141/40 Drain	Type 28 emplacement [2pdr AT gun]
TL497848	Pymore	Type 28 emplacement [6pdr OF gun + bren]
TL580818	B1382, Lots Farm	Type 22 pillbox
TL571814	Queen Adelaide	Type 28 emplacement [6pdr OF + bren]
TL570817	Queen Adelaide	rectangular pillbox with integral looped blastwall

TL549793	Ely, Causeway Fm.	Type 22 pillbox with two rear loops
TL532727	Dimmocks Cote	Type 22 pillbox
TL495640	River Cam	shellproof, hexagonal pillbox, one of a pair
TL470592	Cambridge	Type 28 emplacement [2pdr AT gun + bren]
TL491595	Cambridge Airport	sunken hexagonal pillbox with loop over entrance
TL478485	Whittlesford Mill	Type 28 emplacement [2pdr AT gun + bren]
TL498440	Ickleton	rectangular pillbox with rear, looped blastwall
TL455465	RAF Duxford	hexagonal pillbox with 7 loops & sunken entrance
TL402667	RAF Oakington	FCConstruction pillbox
TL412674	RAF Oakington	hexagonal pillbox with extra observation loops
TL659658	RAF Snailwell	hexagonal pillbox with thickening to loop height
TL300796	RAF Warboys	FCConstruction pillbox
TL278750	RAF Wyton	square pillbox with half-height blastwall
TL525809	Ely, Beald Drove	Type 22 pillbox
TL295859	Ramsey	Type 22 pillbox on plinth above stream
TL183606	St Neots	Type 22 pillbox on Mill Common
TL393749	Earith	Allan-Williams turret on Earith Bulwark

ROYAL OBSERVER CORPS POSTS

TL135994	Castor	underground monitoring post
TF095379	Parson Drove	underground monitoring post
TL430502	Harston	underground monitoring post

SPIGOT MORTAR PEDESTALS

TF458098	Wisbech	behind rugby clubhouse
TF430062	River Nene	north bank opposite A47, east of Guyhirn
TF279050	Thorney	next to anti-tank emplacement, Bukehorn Road
TF396032	Guyhirn	by Murrow road covering former rail bridge
TF399024	Rings End	between A141 and former railway
TIL262924	Pondersbridge	alongside B1040 road, moved from original site
TL275998	Dog-in-a-Doublet	next to pillbox north of bridge
TL315977	Coates	overturned beside A605
TL576877	Littleport	in river bank, A1101 north of level crossing
TL553873	Littleport	south of All 01 road to Wisbech
TL545795	Ely	on river bank covering A142 road bridge
TL543795	Ely	beside A142 covering level-crossing
TL392748	Earith	beside Civil War fort near Allan-Williams turret
TL395746	Earith	in marina covering A1123 river crossing
TL431680	Rampton	in earthworks of Giant's Hill, mediaeval castle
TL501644	Waterbeach	two pedestals covering crossing of Cam

PLACES TO VISIT

Imperial War Museum DUXFORD-. an almost complete Expansion Period airfield with earlier hangars and other structures from the Great War, also a collection of air-raid shelters, a coast defence gun, and other relevant exhibits.

LITTLE STAUGHTON is an almost complete example of a wartime airfield with most of its buildings intact, much is visible from public roads since it is now an industrial estate.

Many working airfields such as BASSINGBOURN, MOLESWORTH, OAKINGTON, WATERBEACH, WITTERING, and WYTON are visible from public roads. Others, like BOURN, CASTLE CAMPS, GRANSDEN LODGE, NEWMARKET HEATH, WITCHFORD and WRATTING COMMON are used for agricultural or industrial purposes, and are, again, visible from public roads.

Most of the anti-invasion defences listed in the Gazetteer are accessible from public roads, footpaths, riverbanks and so on. Particularly interesting groups of defences may be seen:

between Speechley's Drove [TF218061] and the River Welland [TF202090]
from Stone Bridge Corner [TF277009] to Dog-in-a-Doublet [TF274994]
at TL329913 above Benwick to Floods Ferry [TL357927]
at Pymore [TL480852,498847,497848,and 499849]
on the bank of the River Cam [TL495640 and 494638]
at Queen Adelaide [TL571814, 570817, 580818, 576817]